# COLLABORATIVE LEARNING
## Pocketbook

**By Gael Luzet**

Cartoons:
Phil Hailstone

Published by:

**Teachers' Pocketbooks**
Laurel House, Station Approach,
Alresford, Hampshire SO24 9JH, UK
Tel: +44 (0)1962 735573
Fax: +44 (0)1962 733637
Email: sales@teacherspocketbooks.co.uk
Website: www.teacherspocketbooks.co.uk

Teachers' Pocketbooks is an imprint of
Management Pocketbooks Ltd.

Series editor – Linda Edge

© Gael Luzet 2013

This edition published 2013
ISBN 978 1 906610 47 0

E-book ISBN 978 1 908282 99 0

British Library Cataloguing-in-Publication Data
– A catalogue record for this book is available
from the British Library.

Design, artwork and graphics by Efex Ltd.
Printed in UK.

# Contents

# Foreword

> I really like it when we can talk in class...

...says Kelly in Year 8, grinning from ear to ear (and revealing the bright pink gum she seems to be constantly chewing behind my back) when I suggest a group activity on a grey Monday morning. Although I suspect that she might like it for the wrong reasons, I know that there is a lot for her – and the other 29 students in the class – to learn in a structured co-operative learning context.

And the truth is, as a teacher, I *really* like it too!

# Foreword

This Pocketbook on collaborative learning is aimed at teachers with an interest in developing **small group work** amongst pupils. The strategies and practical examples described here have all been given the seal of approval by classroom practitioners who believe in a more cohesive classroom culture than didactic teaching traditionally provides. The book focuses on small-scale classroom co-operation – a subset of collaborative activities and interactions that actively engage learners and lead to great outcomes.

There are, of course, other kinds of collaborative learning than group work, notably communities of enquiry, whole class projects and, increasingly, technology-based options incorporating, for example, social media and virtual worlds. While they all have an exciting place in modern education, they fall outside the scope of this book.

'I didn't like group work at first because I didn't know the other students. Now I enjoy it more because I feel more confident. In my group, we help each other and we get on really well!' **Simran in Year 6**

'With group work, you learn a lot about students; the way they learn and interact with each other, etc. It gives you a chance to step back and, hand over ownership of the lesson to the students.' **Mary, secondary Spanish teacher**

'Group work is fun. I get more work done in a group than by myself. It's less stressful as well because the teacher doesn't stare at you from the front!' **Michael in Year 9**

'The teacher is able to sit with one group while the others work collaboratively in their groups. It's an opportunity to focus on children who may need help to participate and share their ideas.' **Anushka, Year 5 teacher**

# The Power of More Than One

# Welcome

Welcome to the world of collaborative learning.

You may be new to this place, eager to find out what collaborative learning is all about; or a returning visitor in quest of fresh ideas. Whatever your circumstances, a journey into the collaborative world will bring you wealth and excitement... At least in terms of teaching!

# Meet Karl...

Karl is the archetypal resident of the collaborative learning world. An average eleven-year-old boy, Karl has learnt and been taught the collaborative way for several years. Here is what Karl, our model collaborative learner, looks like:

Able to verbalise and communicate his thoughts

Good awareness and management of his own emotions

Enjoys project-based learning and sets himself learning goals (with guidance from his teacher)

Respectful of others and able to assimilate his own personal success with the success of the group

Good active listening skills

Equipped with the necessary problem-solving and decision-making tools

Keen to learn in partnership with others

# ...Now that you have met him

Which of us wouldn't want Karl in our class!

If you like the idea of a collaborative classroom culture (one that fosters learners like Karl) and would like to find out more, you've picked up the right book. It will:

- Define and explain collaborative learning and demonstrate the benefits of working together
- Help you plan effectively for collaborative learning
- Provide a wealth of practical ideas, big and small, for successful group learning
- Present methods of assessing and evaluating

# Defining collaborative learning

**What is collaborative learning?**
Collaborative learning refers to an engineered situation in which two or more people learn together. Although they depend on each other for the successful completion of a task, learners also remain accountable for their own learning.

**What is it not?**
Collaborative learning is not just a setting technique. Organising learners into groups does not guarantee that learning will take place. In fact, grouping can sometimes be detrimental to learning; it can lead to disengagement, disagreement or even disruption.

Therefore, like all good teaching strategies, collaborative learning relies on meticulous planning and careful delivery. As for the learners, their readiness to learn is the golden key to the collaborative treasure chest and its wealth of benefits for everyone involved.

# Collaborative vs co-operative

The terms '**collaborative**' and '**co-operative**' are both used to describe working together in groups. Are they the same thing?

Educationalists such as John Myers (*Co-operative Learning*, 1991) point out that dictionary definitions of 'collaboration', derived from its Latin root, focus on the *process* of working together whereas the etymology of 'co-operation' stresses the *product* of such work. As a result, collaboration may demand an even greater degree of independence from the teacher than co-operation does.

It's an interesting distinction but, setting aside the academic debate, collaborative and co-operative learning are fundamentally similar. Both:

- Favour active student participation over passive lecture-based teaching
- Require a specific task to be completed

In an endeavour to focus on practical classroom strategies I have used the terms interchangeably throughout this book, along with the more generic classroom-friendly '**group work**'.

# Historical roots

Learning together is clearly not a new thing. Ancient civilisations often encouraged individuals to learn from one another. In the Academy founded by Plato in ancient Athens, students were given problems to solve amongst themselves through a **dialogical process**.

In the 19th century, when schooling became compulsory in a large number of countries, the idea of learning from one another was relegated in favour of what we now consider to be the traditional methodology: the **sage-on-stage** approach, where the teacher hands out knowledge from the front of the classroom.

Interest in collaborative learning rose again in the 1980s, following the worldwide publication of Lev Vygotsky's work on social development. Vygotsky, a developmental theorist and researcher who worked in 1920s and 30s Soviet Russia, has influenced some of the current research on teacher-student co-operation and on the role of cultural learning in children's development.

# Vygotskian theory

One of the recurrent themes in Vygotsky's **Social Development Theory**, along with the idea that social history (culture) influences intellectual functioning, is that 'the one who does the talking does the learning'.

Vygotsky explains that social interaction precedes development. Consciousness and cognition are the end products of socialisation and social behaviour. In other words, children learn from interacting with the adults and other children around them. It's a compelling idea that resonates loudly in teaching.

The 'power of more than one' forms the theoretical backbone of collaborative learning.

> 'The one who does the talking does the learning'
> **Lev Vygotsky**

# Vygotskian theory in action!

*When my daughter was two, I sat with her in front of a jigsaw puzzle. She eagerly tried to force random pieces together, until I showed her where and how to place them, while modelling the intellectual process orally: 'This piece is not the right shape so let's try and put it somewhere else'.*

*Two years later, she is telling her 16-month-old brother how to put a jigsaw puzzle together. The same pattern of language is emerging. My daughter has internalised and reproduced the scaffolded instructions that were probably passed on to me by my parents. And, miraculously, my baby boy seems to have come round to the idea that jigsaw pieces have another function than just teething aids.*

This example illustrates how learning springs naturally from social interaction. It happens the moment one individual engages verbally with another. Talking *is* teaching and learning.

Besides, researchers have observed that when students work together on complex tasks, they help each other in much the same way that adults help children (or older siblings assist younger ones). In such tasks, dialogue consists of mutual regulation. Together, learners can solve difficult problems that they cannot solve working independently.

# Zone of Proximal Development

Vygotsky argues that effective learning occurs – with guidance and encouragement from a knowledgeable person – somewhere in between what is known and what is unknown by the learner. He calls this the **Zone of Proximal Development (ZPD)**.

The knowledgeable person can be a teacher, or a parent, or another member of the peer group who has additional skills, knowledge or information. As the diagram shows, social interaction, scaffolding and a good set of collaborative skills (as described in the next section) form the basis of effective group learning.

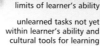

**Teacher or Peer**

**Learner**

assisted learning

INTERACTION

scaffold

learned tasks

unlearned tasks at limits of learner's ability

unlearned tasks not yet within learner's ability and cultural tools for learning

Zone of proximal development

# ZPD and peer-led development

As teachers, we need to bear in mind the implications of Vygotsky's Zone of Proximal Development when designing collaborative learning tasks.

To guarantee engagement, accessibility and challenge, whatever task we set has to be carefully placed within the boundaries of our learners' ZPD. If the task is too difficult, the bridge of social interaction will collapse; too easy, and the bridge will become redundant – students will not need each other's help to complete the task.

Where a task sits comfortably in the ZPD, **peer-led development**, which allows pupils to learn through interaction as well as observation, will occur naturally.

We know from Vygotsky's research that children's conceptual development is aided by the acceptance and adjustment processes to which they subject themselves in effective group work. Hearing the different views of others who are at the same level of intellectual and emotional development can lead to a noticeable boost in progress.

# Peer-led development process

The diagram below illustrates the straightforward setting for peer-led development. 'The instructor' is at one end of the process; and the product – a target for the group to aim for – at the other. During the process, the instructor will wear several different hats, becoming, in turn, motivator, facilitator and assessor.

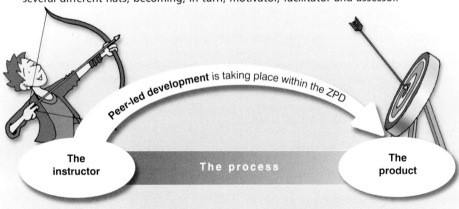

Peer-led development is taking place within the ZPD

**The instructor**

**The process**

**The product**

# Peer-led development process

**The instructor**
This is likely to be you, the teacher, but could be a teaching assistant or a fellow student. Alternatively (or additionally), you can provide the group with **written** or **recorded instructions**.

**The process**
Individuals within the group bring their own set of **collaborative skills** to the task (see following chapter). They have ownership of the task and are responsible, both individually and co-operatively, for its success. They encourage one another. Through discussion, mediation and problem-solving they pull each other out of their **zone of acquired knowledge** and into the **zone of new knowledge**.

**The product**
The product can be a design, a problem solved, an experiment, a piece of writing, etc… and is always accompanied by a set of **clear success criteria**.

# Motivational benefits of group work

On many levels, learning with others is a source of stimulation. There's a parallel with team sport, where success is dependent on the ability to 'pull together'. When carefully implemented, collaborative learning provides opportunities to:

- Bring pupils together and develop a team spirit
- Encourage cross-pupil support
- Add a competitive dimension to a task (groups competing against each other)
- Repair a damaged relationship between teacher and pupils

This last bullet point is important. Repairing a damaged relationship is tricky. Group work can help insofar as it deflects pupils' attention from the teacher, who can then take the opportunity to talk to difficult students away from the gaze of others. Pupils with challenging behaviour get to interact more with their peers which shifts their focus from the personal conflict to the group's objectives.

# Cognitive benefits of group work

In a group setting, all kinds of learning styles and abilities collide. It is precisely this exposure to other people's cognitive skills that benefits individual learners.

Group work gives your students a chance to reach **higher levels of reasoning** in **open-ended, creative tasks**. Co-operatively, they might have to work out causes and effects, deconstruct information, categorise and form hypotheses, solve problems, negotiate and reach common decisions. It teaches them to think deeply and laterally.

It also teaches them that 'the answer' does not always have to come from the teacher or the textbook!

# The teacher-facilitator

As a by-product of Vygotskian theory, teaching in a collaborative setting demands a fresh look at the role of the teacher. A colleague recently observed:

> *I like group work in the sense that it shifts the limelight away from me as a teacher. The only thing is ... ... I feel a bit redundant. I have this urge to ask students questions, to interrupt and explain what they have probably already worked out as a group. It makes me realise how much of a power freak I am in the classroom!*

Teachers in training are taught to – and expected to – lead from the front. This seems to be the default setting of a (good) teacher. No one can deny the importance of didactic teaching and this book certainly does not advocate its abolition. However, there is a danger with traditional pedagogy of losing sight of discovery and self-directed learning, two invaluable experiences that many students will be required to turn into professional skills.

At the heart of collaborative learning is the **teacher-facilitator**, not an omnipotent imparter of knowledge but an architect of learning who carefully plans and monitors the process. The teacher-facilitator subscribes to the idea that group work creates independent thinkers and effective learners.

# Benefits for the teacher-facilitator

'To me group work is about equality of treatment: everyone gets a chance to work at their own pace in their own way, as long as the objectives are met at the end of the lesson... and there's no teacher's pet either!'
**Craig, Year 4 teacher**

'It can help with diffusion of conflict. If a student struggles with authority, he or she may feel more comfortable working with peers. And the teacher gets to relax a bit more as well...'
**Ian, secondary Science teacher**

'The amount of informal assessment I get during group projects is fantastic! I walk around with my mark book, note down observations and targets which I use for student reviews, parents evenings, etc...'
**Claire, secondary Art teacher**

'For me, it is all about the process in group work. The end result is secondary in a way... I like to see my students positively engaged with each other. They learn real life skills: how to persuade, how to let go, how to listen and wait for their turn to speak, etc...'.
**Katrina, secondary Music teacher**

# Conclusion

Collaborative learning complements and enhances didactic teaching. Inside the ZPD, learners make progress with the help of a more knowledgeable facilitator, a **guide on the side** who paves the way and encourages them at every step.

As a teacher-facilitator, you are always there to help; you set the task and review the outcome; you observe, steer, motivate, correct. You unlock and manage the 'power of more than one'.

So now it's time to roll up your sleeves: the next section of this book will provide you with guidance on planning effectively for collaborative learning.

# Planning for Collaborative Learning

# Why bother?

A teacher relates his experience of group work:

> 'I ask them to get into groups of four. They start to squabble and it takes a good ten minutes for them to get sorted. Then I look around the room: two shy girls are sitting together by my desk, looking mortified; the rest of the class is re-arranged in three groups of four, one group of five and, at the back of the room, the usual suspects – six of them squeezed around a single table, having an animated chat about some TV programme last night. And I can't help but think: 'Why do I bother?''

That teacher was me in my first year of teaching, failing miserably to implement a strategy that my Head of Department encouraged. I was being naïve, of course. Letting students who are unfamiliar with this way of working sit in friendship groups is asking for trouble. Since then I've learnt that successful collaborative learning requires careful planning.

# What to expect

The following pages will:

* Help you set up for collaborative learning   ground rules, **group size, group composition**
* Offer **strategies** to deal with reluctant participants
* Look at the **key collaborative skills** your students need to acquire

Collaborative learning may take up part of your lesson, the whole of it, or be conducted over a series of lessons. It can be employed in a wide variety of contexts with all age groups. Although young children inevitably lack maturity and experience, it is beneficial to start group work as early as possible in order to develop the four basic collaborative skills mentioned on page 43.

Used strategically, collaborative learning supports your long-term teaching and learning objectives: exploring a new topic, gathering information or data, analysing, problem-solving and evaluating. It works best when higher-order thinking is required, and when the task is open-ended and interpretive.

# Initial steps

Some children, particularly younger ones, may not straight away see the point of working together as a group. After all, school judges them on their individual merits, not on their ability to get on with each other! Group work can also make some children feel insecure, even threatened (more on that coming up). So how can you motivate them to take part in collaborative learning?

**STEP 1**

Take the time to talk to your class about **why and how group work is useful** – use the material from the previous section on 'the power of more than one' to support you. Let students contribute their thoughts and ideas too.

**STEP 2**

Discuss **success criteria** with them (What does success in group work look like?)

**STEP 3**

Ask students to design a common set of **ground rules** that will apply to all future collaborative tasks.

# Success criteria

Clearly-defined success criteria that offer enough scope for pupils at both ends of the learning spectrum to thrive will ensure motivation and achievement all round.

Once a group task has been outlined, **show an example** of the finished work or model product. This is especially helpful to lower attainers who might struggle to generate their own success criteria. Some pupils need to 'see' what quality looks like before giving it a try themselves. Also, brainstorm with your class **factors affecting success**. These might include: engagement; leadership; peer support; perseverance; the ability to compromise and subdivide tasks; the quality of explanation and evaluation. They all rely heavily on mastery of the **four key collaborative skills** described later in this section.

Build **differentiation** into the group task by describing learning objectives in terms of what learners *must*, *should* and *could* achieve. One MFL teacher wanted his students to understand what makes a good group role-play. He showed them a video of former students in groups of three performing an excellent role-play. He then described the learning objectives. All groups:

- **Must** understand what makes a good role-play in the target language
- **Should** be able to suggest improvements to the videoed role-play
- **Could** produce (and perform) their own script based on the one they studied together

# Setting the ground rules

Give your students a chance to discuss and agree as a whole class a **shared set of ground rules** for collaborative learning. These should be clearly displayed in the classroom and adhered to at all times. They will ensure consistency across all groups, regardless of size or composition. Examples:

- Listen to each other in a sympathetic way
- Always take it in turns to speak
- Encourage everyone to contribute
- Never put people down
- Focus on the task and don't get distracted
- Friendship does not matter; the success of the group does
- Say how you feel but don't point the finger at anyone

It is perfectly acceptable for you to act as referee and to intervene when a ground rule is breached. However, as students become more experienced and refine their collaborative learning skills, they will begin to self-regulate, allowing you to step back.

# Low noise and zero noise signals

Unmanaged noise can become a real problem in a collaborative learning situation. Of course, there should be a healthy buzz in your classroom while students work together. It will reflect their excitement for the task and their engagement in a learning conversation. But it can get out of hand. Establish in advance a clear system of signals to manage the noise level during group activities.

A **zero noise signal** is an easy way to 'freeze' the class and focus students' attention on you when you need to give instructions or provide clarification. You could use a raised hand or a flag. If you prefer a sound signal, try a whistle or clap your hands five times to get everyone's attention.

It is also helpful to have a different signal (audio or visual) to indicate that the noise level is too high. It helps if you teach your students to use a '6 inch voice' (a level of volume appropriate for a listener who is 6 inches away) and use your **low voice signal** to bring the decibels down to an acceptable level.

# Does size matter?

Think carefully about group size when planning co-operative tasks. It has to fit the learning purpose. As a general rule, the smaller the group the more manageable it is. The following grid describes the advantages and disadvantages of various group sizes and suggests the kinds of activities that best fit:

| GROUP SIZE | ADVANTAGES | DISADVANTAGES |
|---|---|---|
| **Pair** | • More likely to guarantee pupil involvement<br>• Ownership of learning equally shared<br>• Good for peer assessment and peer evaluation<br>• Helps build confidence<br>• *Free rider*[1] behaviour very unlikely | • Possible reluctance in non-friendship groups<br>• Too easy in lower-order thinking activities (simple tasks) |
| **Three** | • Ideal for practising decision-making and consensus<br>• Shared ownership of learning<br>• Good setting for complex tasks demanding higher-order thinking<br>• *Free rider*[1] behaviour unlikely | • One pupil can dominate<br>• One pupil can be left out |

[1] *Free rider* behaviour, as defined by Baines, Blatchford and Kutnick (2009):
*'when a member lets others do all the work'.*

# Does size matter?

| | | |
|---|---|---|
| **Four or five** | • Good for group discussions and problem solving tasks<br>• Good for investigation and research<br>• Helps bring together a range of views<br>• Development of 'team spirit' (competitive dimension) | • Risk of group subdividing into two<br>• Can be intimidating for pupils lacking confidence<br>• Increased risk of *free rider*[1] behaviour and diffusion of responsibility |
| **Six or more** | • Good for surveys and gathering information<br>• Development of 'team spirit' (competitive dimension)<br>• Works better when led by an adult or very competent student | • Risk of group subdividing into two or more<br>• Can be daunting for younger learners and pupils lacking confidence<br>• High risk of *free rider*[1] behaviour and diffusion of responsibility |

[1] *Free rider* behaviour, as defined by Baines, Blatchford and Kutnick (2009): *'when a member lets others do all the work'.*

# Gender and ability groupings

As a general rule, **heterogeneous grouping** – ie groups of mixed ability and gender – works better. In heterogeneous groups where trust is embedded, high achievers support less able pupils by offering guidance and demonstrating effective thought processes. Mixed ability grouping provides inherent differentiation and support. It also encourages all types of learners to interact and form positive relationships.

**Homogeneous grouping** is based on selection criteria set by the teacher. Depending on the work you have planned, you may want to put all the boys in one group and the girls in another, or to organise groups according to ability or talents. If you have a minority of boys in your class, for instance, especially in the early teenage years, they may benefit from (and appreciate) the chance to work as a group from time to time. A table of weaker students working with a teaching assistant who can break down, model and explain the work is sometimes a good option. And occasionally putting your best students together with access to a wider range of material and specialist information will be appropriate.

# Friendship grouping

It's best to avoid **friendship groups** (at least at the start of your collaborative journey) if you don't want to have to deal with the situation described at the start of this section. It takes a mature and self-motivated learner to resist the temptation of off-task behaviour in a friendship group, especially when students are in threes or more. The opportunity to socialise is likely to get in the way of the work. Friends also tend to be of the same sex and ability, so grouping them together does not foster an inclusive ethos.

However, friendship has one significant advantage over all other types of grouping: trust already exists amongst members of the group. Friends are also better equipped at dealing with conflict and are less likely to fall out if they struggle to reach an agreement.

Friendship groups can only work once the class has gained a positive view of collaborative learning and a degree of experience. Even so, have strategies ready to deal with 'off-task' behaviour, such as a countdown device to remind students regularly of the time remaining to complete their task. Also, listen in on group discussions to monitor how well the established ground rules are being followed.

# Grouping by role

Many children enjoy role-play and it's a technique that lends itself well to group work. Try assigning a role to each member of a group to increase engagement, promote collaboration and improve the effectiveness of the group. So that they develop a wider range of skills, ensure that students aren't always allocated the same type of role.

It's useful to have a few sets of **'job description' cards** to hand out to your class when you decide to assign roles. Each card briefly describes what the student will have to undertake within his or her group. On those cards, the outcome of the collaborative task is referred to as 'the product'. You will need to make this explicit to your students. If you decide to get a team to present their product to the rest of the class, ask the leader to be spokesperson (unless the leader prefers to share the burden of public speaking with others in the team!).

### Scribe
You must take clear notes on what the group discusses and decides. You then have to write up your notes for the final product.

### Reader
You must read out the instructions to the group. Make sure everyone understands what they have to do. Check that they are doing it properly.

# Job description cards

### Leader
You must make sure everyone does what they have to do. Keep an eye on the clock, ensure the group is working well and help wherever it is needed.

### Coach
You are the Leader's second in command. Encourage everyone to take part. Motivate the team to work well together and help wherever it is needed.

### Researcher
Your job is to gather facts and information. Use a range of resources and present your findings to the team.

### Technician
You are in charge of the tools and materials needed for the task. Give them out to the right people and assist in using them.

### Designer
Your job is to design the format in which to present the product. You are in charge of the layout, illustrations and all other visuals.

### Quality controller
You have to check the quality of the product. Ensure the product meets the success criteria set by your teacher at the start of the task.

# Competency grouping

An alternative to role grouping is **competency grouping**, which involves organising teams according to individual strengths. Competency grouping is a useful approach in collaborative activities where a varied end product is required. It can be very motivational, allowing people to play to their strengths.

Create groups according to individual members' talents, interests or knowledge. For example, groups may comprise someone who has good oral presentation or drama skills, someone who likes writing, someone who is good at researching information, someone with practical skills and someone with artistic talent who can come up with a design, etc.

You can ask students in advance to identify and rank their strengths – this is useful information that you can draw on throughout the year.

A word of warning though: a possible danger of this technique is to 'pigeonhole' pupils. It can restrict them to their comfort zone and deter them from trying in areas where they need to improve. So apply this technique sparingly to get the best out of it.

# The reluctant group worker

Remember Karl, the collaborative enthusiast described at the beginning of this book? Karl enjoys group work and thrives in a co-operative context but this may not be the case for all of his classmates. What about Molly who never says anything in class? And Maryam who suffers bullying at school? And Max who has speech and language difficulties and needs more time than others to express his thoughts?

Molly

Some people, for many different reasons, simply do not feel at ease in a group setting. Collaborative learning can be a daunting experience for them. As a result, they tend to behave in a detrimental way: some will attempt to distract the group, others will just blend into the background or refuse to contribute.

Maryam

Unfortunately, reluctant or unwilling group workers can cause teachers to shun collaborative learning in favour of more traditional teacher-led methods which are perceived as 'safer'. So what can we do to encourage participation?

Max

# Engaging the reluctant group worker

By and large, children crave acceptance from their peers. The key is to make reluctant pupils see that group work provides an opportunity to achieve this.

There are ways to get around the obstacle posed by those who are less than enthusiastic in group work.

- **Start small!** Get your students used to working in pairs. Ensure that the pairs are balanced and that personalities do not clash. Make it explicit to them that they can achieve much more with a partner than on their own. Use praise to 'glue' the pairs (*I like the way you organised your ideas in two columns; good team decision!*)

- **Use 'snowballing'**, where each pair's work feeds into small group work formed by combining pairs. Reluctant group workers feel safer sharing the responsibility of their input with a partner before feeding it to another pair

# Engaging the reluctant group worker

- **Use stable groups**. The longer the group has been running, the more likely it is to encourage familiarity and trust. Shy students benefit the most from group stability

- **Reinforce individual accountability**. Remind students that the group is only as strong as the sum of its parts. Everyone in the group is held accountable for the success of the task. Highlight this as a fundamental ground rule for group work

- **Allocate roles**. This allows reluctant students to play a defining part in the success of the group task. It is perceived as less threatening since you are 'putting a mask on' when acting as a designer, coach or quality controller. Similarly, if you are being asked to use your expertise as an artist or researcher or public speaker you feel valued and included

# The reluctant group worker's phrase book

Here are the kinds of phrases that your unwilling team worker might use:

'I can't work with...'

'They won't let me...'

'I don't want to'

'Do I have to?'

'I can't be bothered'

'He / she gets on my nerves'

(to a peer) 'Why can't you do it yourself?'

'What is the point of...?'

'Can I go to the toilet (please)?'*

You will have heard similar phrases in your classroom. Beneath the cheeky bluntness that we have come to love (or not!) from our students, there is an underlying issue inherent to the process of growing up: the underdevelopment of social (or collaborative) skills. Working with others is not just about willingness, it is a question of capability.

*Common multi-functional escape phrase, occasionally followed by an emphatic expression such as 'I'm bursting'.*

# The collaborative jigsaw

At the heart of effective collaborative learning is a set of **skills** that your learners need to develop or acquire. They are central to the process of learning together.

The diagram opposite identifies these skills and highlights their interdependence.

**Collaborative Jigsaw**

# Intrapersonal skills

**Intrapersonal skills** are vital to the learning process. They are defined as the ability to hear and analyse your own thoughts. Intrapersonal skills allow you to manage your emotions and sense of self, and are a prerequisite to *inter*personal skills. In a collaborative situation, pupils' *intra*personal intelligence defines their self-belief, which in turn impacts on how they work with others.

Developing your students' intrapersonal skills is all about encouraging self-reflection and boosting their self-confidence. Strictly speaking, you cannot 'teach' intrapersonal skills but you can model them and show your students how important they are in making good personal choices.

# How to develop intrapersonal skills

To encourage the development of intrapersonal skills in your collaborative classroom:

- **Inform your students in advance**. Prior to your collaborative lesson, let your students know the learning objectives, what will happen in the lesson and how it will be achieved. Encourage reflection and incite forward planning by setting a preliminary task, for example a KWL grid (see page 62) to fill in at home

- Give students **space and time to think** before the start of a co-operative task. Allow them to read through the material and maybe fill in a questionnaire about it or mark-up/ highlight text in specific ways before they get into groups to discuss it

- **Model your thought process** to the group using a first-person narrative: *'I am looking at this plant and I am wondering how it grows all the time. Is it something in the air or should I investigate the soil? I know for a fact that the roots need water… …'* Encourage your students to do the same in their groups

- **Model the use of enquiry language**. Use phrases like *'I wonder how'* and *'what I would like to know is'*. Encourage students to pose hypothetical questions which start with *'what if'*, for instance

# Interpersonal skills

As a teacher, you know only too well how some children's poor communication skills affect their well-being at school. In a collaborative setting, a poor communicator can have a detrimental effect on the whole group and can end up with damaged self-esteem. Yet students can only learn effective communication within a social context.

**Interpersonal skills**, which refer to a person's ability to get along and interact successfully with others, underpin group work. Students with good interpersonal skills have a tendency to project a positive attitude and look for solutions to problems. They visibly thrive in a collaborative context. As a teacher-facilitator, it is crucial to help your students understand – and most importantly manage – their relationships with each other within the classroom environment.

# How to develop interpersonal skills

To encourage the development of interpersonal skills in your collaborative classroom:

- Use **'we'** and **'together'** instead of 'you' when explaining the task. This gives an all-inclusive dimension to your instructional language. *'Today we are going to mind-map our research from last week in order to define the notion of fair trade.'*
- Involve students in setting **social** as well as **academic targets** in group activities. *'First of all you should agree as a group on a time scale for this activity to be completed.'*
- Model **empathy** and **negotiating skills** whenever you can. *'Yes, you are right, we should colour-code the sentences that refer to the narrator's feelings in the text.'*
- Monitor pupils' behaviour towards others and their **positive contribution** to the group. You could, for example, hand out a quick self-evaluation form at the end of the lesson where students assess their role in the success of the group task. Praise and reward also provide an incentive to contribute in a positive way
- If necessary, make students **aware of their behaviour** and how it affects others. Needless to say, this has to be done with a degree of sensitivity

# Active listening skills

When we ask children to **listen** or **watch** they tend to hear or see instead. They get the words, but do they get the message? Developing good **active listening skills**, or fully understanding the message, is essential for success when learning with others.

Teach your learners that listening is not a passive activity. It requires concentration and a degree of personal involvement. An active listener has to pay attention to what someone else is saying and show comprehension by using a range of verbal and non-verbal strategies, eg:

- Nodding
- Maintaining eye contact
- Showing empathy
- Shaking head in approval or disgust
- Not interrupting or filling silences
- Responding appropriately (*'That's right'*, *'I agree'*, *'No way!'*, *'Wow!'*, *'Really?'*, *'I like that'*, *'Are you serious?'*, *etc*)
- Paraphrasing
- Seeking clarification and asking for examples (*'What do you mean?'*, *'What happened?'*, *'What did you say?'*, *'Can you show me how?'*, *etc*)

# How to develop active listening skills

To encourage the development of active listening skills in your collaborative classroom:

* Get your students, in pairs, to **role-play the effects of not listening**. While one of the students is telling a story, the other shows a blatant lack of interest or a distracted attitude (yawning, pretending to check their phone, fiddling with their pencil case, not making eye contact, looking bored, interrupting, etc…). Then the students swap roles. Ask them how it feels not to be listened to. How should a good listener behave instead? A list of good listening attributes could be drawn up and displayed for everyone to see

* **Evaluate pupils' listening ability**. Share with them good listening tips, including what gets in the way of effective listening. Give them an individual or a team score which reflects their capacity to be attentive and sensitive to others. Reward their effort

* Choose a mildly controversial issue and ask your students to **take it in turn to present their opinion**. All group members take notes, writing down the gist of what the speaker is saying until it is their turn to talk. At the end of the process, the group can synthesise all the different views into a mind map or a narrative entitled *'What we think of… '*

# Speaking skills

Over the last 20 years, increased emphasis has been placed on effective talk amongst pupils. To improve their **speaking skills**, your students need a clear framework for interaction. Like the other three basic skills in the collaborative jigsaw puzzle, speaking is a prerequisite to any form of classroom collaboration.

Speaking is the main medium of communication in group work, where decisions are always taken and problems are always solved orally. In a group situation, students need to be confident about enunciating ideas and expressing opinions. Doing this in front of an audience makes the act of speaking so much more interesting for some and quite daunting for others.

# How to develop speaking skills

To encourage the development of speaking skills in your collaborative classroom:

- **Create a positive environment** for speaking, where all learners understand and apply the principle of inclusion. Award your students with a degree of freedom to express personal views, as long as they respect those of others in return
- Allow shy or inexperienced students to provide **minimal responses** at first. Help them build up a stock of minimal responses that they can use in different types of exchanges (agreeing, disagreeing, questioning, deducing, etc…). You can also use a simple voting technique to seek consensus and survey opinions within the group
- Encourage your students to give more **detailed explanations** (*'What do you actually mean by…?' 'Can you tell me a bit more about…?'*) and praise them for clearly getting their meaning across. They will start to develop persuasive skills and gain confidence as a result
- Teach your students to **bounce ideas off** their group (*'What do you reckon, Sam?', 'How does that sound?'*). Nominate a person to monitor the process and check that key ideas are taken up by at least one other person before the group is allowed to move on

# Advanced collaborative skills

Intrapersonal, interpersonal, speaking and active listening skills form the trunk of the collaborative learning tree.

Much more than just a set of attributes for effective classroom co-operation, they are essential lifelong skills. Once empowered with those skills – even at a basic level of competence – your pupils will start to operate efficiently in collaborative mode.

Advanced collaborative skills

INTRAPERSONAL
INTERPERSONAL
ACTIVE LISTENING
SPEAKING

# Advanced collaborative skills

The collaborative tree bears much fruit; you'll find numerous additional benefits grow from it! Better communication will allow your pupils to develop more advanced skills, such as:

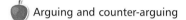 Arguing and counter-arguing    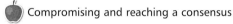 Compromising and reaching a consensus

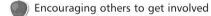 Encouraging others to get involved    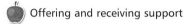 Offering and receiving support

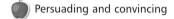 Persuading and convincing     Summarising and drawing conclusions

 Evaluating each other's contribution (peer-assessment)

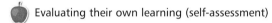 Evaluating their own learning (self-assessment)

The best group outcomes, you will notice, are systematically produced by the most effective teams (and not necessarily the most academic ones). Encourage teams with a strong collaborative track record to send a member '*on loan*' to another group for a one-off session to help them grow their own key collaborative skills.

# Conclusion

Forewarned is forearmed.

Good collaborative learning is all about planning. Putting students together in a group does not guarantee that learning will take place (remember my first attempt at group work?). You have to prepare your students for it. The more experienced and skilled they become, the more likely they are to enjoy and benefit from group work.

You also need to prepare yourself. Draw up your own checklist when planning for collaborative learning. Include:

- Lesson objectives
- Projected outcomes
- Skills needed
- Resources needed
- Ground rules
- Group size
- Group composition
- Group roles
- Support and challenge opportunities

# Collaborative
# Learning
# Starter Pack

# Introduction

Armed with the background knowledge from the previous chapters, you are now ready to rocket-launch into the collaborative stratosphere. This section will equip you with low maintenance yet powerful ideas to boost your practice.

All strategies described in this chapter will help foster a collaborative culture and encourage cohesion in your classroom. Adaptable to all subjects and topics, they are 'quick and easy' group activities designed to support your teaching objectives and fit readily within your lesson plan. They may only take up a small amount of your lesson time but their impact is significant.

Tried and tested in many primary and secondary classrooms, these 'pocket-size' strategies demand minimal preparation. Used to improve thinking and enquiry skills, they also encourage 'proximal development', the process of learning with and from others.

# Get equipped!

 It's worth investing in a few A1 flipcharts – they're useful for a wide range of collaborative activities.

You'll also make good use of the following:

- Scissors and glue
- Colour pencils
- Long rulers for mind maps and graphic organisers
- Sticky labels (on which to write pupils' roles, for instance)
- Egg timers for groups to keep a check on the time
- A set of number holders for your group tables
- A whistle to get your students' attention
- A digital camera to take shots of your team learners at work (use photographs to create collaborative displays)

# Basic collaborative strategies

Common classroom strategies like the ones described here are good starting points for promoting and embedding a more collaborative approach in class:

### 1. Brainstorming
A large or small group activity that encourages students to focus on a topic and contribute to the free flow of ideas. One of the least threatening group strategies, as contributions are generally accepted without criticism. This technique requires a scribe to note down ideas and concepts.

### 3. Snowballing
As with Think-Pair-Share, students work on their own and are then paired up to compare notes, collate findings or write up answers. Two pairs get together and repeat the process. Fours become eights, etc…

### 2. Think-Pair-Share
A short and relatively low-risk collaborative framework. The teacher poses a challenging or open-ended question and gives students time to think about it individually. Students then pair up to discuss and amend their answer. Students are much more willing to share their answer with the teacher or the whole class after they have had a chance to validate it with a classmate.

# How do they work?

Both *Think-Pair-Share* and *Snowballing* include working alone initially.
**Individual thinking** is crucial here and comes before collaborative procedures (we saw in the previous chapter how *intrapersonal* skills precede *interpersonal* ones).

For peer learning to occur, having the time to reflect and formulate a personal response is important. Sharing your personal response with others is enriching, as you get a chance to hear their thoughts and they get a chance to hear yours. It can be both comforting and motivating when you realise that your partner understands and/or agrees with you – and illuminating and challenging when they don't.

*Think-Pair-Share* and *Snowballing* are central communication tools in the modern collaborative classroom. They allow your students to develop or fine-tune their **basic collaborative skills**. *Brainstorming* works on a comparable principle. Everyone can contribute and answers are usually not rejected. It's a safe and easy way to participate in group discussions.

# Placemat

This group activity is a nice alternative to traditional brainstorming, and has the added advantage of increased thinking time. It encourages active listening and group decision-making. Imagine this **placemat** diagram to be on a piece of A2 or A1 paper. Pupils in groups of four sit one on each side of the 'placemat'.

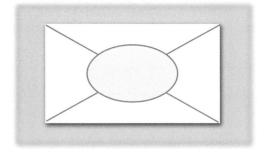

- **Phase 1**. Each group member uses one of the outer spaces to record their thoughts, ideas or responses to the stimulus
- **Phase 2**. Commonly agreed responses are then collated in the inner circle

The co-operative dimension of this exercise springs from the discussion that takes place in the second phase. Members of the group are expected to use key collaborative skills, such as listening carefully to each other, selecting relevant points and reaching agreements.

# Placemats in action

| Key Stage: | Subject / Topic: | Estimated duration: |
|:---:|:---:|:---:|
| **KS2** | **History** | **15-20 mins (including a short video)** |

Mrs Oldendays teaches a History lesson on the daily life of children in the UK during the Second World War. At the start of her lesson, she places students in heterogeneous groups of four and hands out a **placemat** to each quartet.

She shows her pupils a short video with archive images highlighting issues such as rationing, evacuation, sleeping in air raid shelters, etc. She then asks them to write down on their allocated section of the placemat the everyday **challenges** and **problems** that confronted children in the Second World War. She shows them the video one more time.

In phase 2, pupils discuss what that they have noted down individually. Mrs Oldendays asks them to agree on an order of importance (from the biggest challenge / problem to the smallest one) and to record their agreed ranking in the centre of the diagram. Each group then feeds back to the class.

# KWL

KWL provides a great framework for exploring a new topic. Students in groups of two to four are given a grid at the start of a new unit of work.

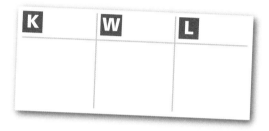

- **K** stands for **Know**. What do we know about this topic? This is the **prior knowledge activation** question
- **W** stands for **Want**. What do we want (or need) to know about this topic?
- **L** stands for **Learnt**. What have we learnt about this topic? This last column is the review section of the KWL grid which can be completed at the end of the topic as a plenary or self-evaluation tool

This type of graphic organiser allows learners to visualise their learning journey, from prior to newly acquired knowledge. It helps them see the bigger picture, the connections within a topic and the progress they are making in the subject.

# KWL in action

| Key Stage: | Subject / Topic: | Estimated duration: |
|---|---|---|
| **KS1** | **Dinosaurs** | **15 mins at start of topic + 15 mins at end** |

Mr Flint has just introduced the new topic to his class: dinosaurs. His pupils are sitting in tables of four or five. He hands out a **KWL** grid on A3 paper to each table. The title at the top of the sheet is 'Dinosaurs'.

He asks each table to discuss what they already know about dinosaurs (K). One pupil per table writes it down in the grid. Pupils then discuss what they want to know about dinosaurs (W). Another group member writes down a list of questions that the group would like answered. The last column is left blank until the unit of work is completed. Mr Flint collects the grids and displays them on his classroom wall.

At the end of the topic pupils return to their KWL grids. They discuss the questions they originally identified in the W column. Can they answer them now? They write their answers in the L (*learnt*) column and add in any extra information they have acquired.

# Numbered heads together

*'Numbered heads together'* is a collaborative learning technique which holds each student accountable for the outcome of a task.

1. In groups of four, students are allocated a number (from 1 to 4).
2. The teacher asks a question, and then tells the students in each team to *put their heads together* to come up with a full answer.
3. When the teacher calls out a number, students with that number raise their hands to respond.

This instructional strategy is used to activate prior knowledge and assess mastery. It fosters active participation and creates a more supportive ethos or 'team spirit' amongst your groups. Pupils tend to see *'numbered heads together'* as low risk due to the collective answering required. Supported by others in their group, students with learning difficulties benefit well from this technique.

*'Numbered heads together'* works best in situations where the question posed demands careful consideration. Allow groups to reach a consensus before calling out a number. Make it competitive, fast-paced and fun. This easy-to-set-up classroom strategy is particularly handy when you need to energise your troops on a grey Monday morning!

# Numbered heads together in action

| Key Stage: | Subject / Topic: | Estimated duration: |
|:---:|:---:|:---:|
| **KS3** | **Maths** | **30 mins** |

Mrs Cardinal divides her Year 7 class into seven groups of four. As a revision activity for the end-of-topic test on comparing probabilities, she decides to give them a series of problems to solve. In each group, students are randomly allocated a number from 1 to 4. Together they work out how to solve the problems.

When Mrs Cardinal wants to hear the answer to a problem, she calls out a number. All students with that number must be able to provide and explain the solution on behalf of their group. She uses *'numbered heads together'* as a way to ensure that all members remain focused on the task, as well as accountable for the success of their group.

# Double-entry journals

The purpose of a double-entry journal is to give your learners an opportunity to express their thoughts and become more involved with material they are studying – anything from a fiction or non-fiction text to a song or magazine advert.

Double-entry journals require minimal preparation time and resources. A piece of A4 paper divided into two columns will do. The left-hand column is for quotations **directly extracted from the source material**, while the right-hand column is for **pupils' individual responses** to those extracts. Double-entry journals provide an opportunity for your learners to choose what is important to them and to provide a personal reading of the source material.

When used as a small group activity (ideally with students in threes), double-entry journals offer a chance for group members to **compare individual interpretations**.

You can add a third column called *'group consensus'* where the team agrees or disagrees with the statements made by each of its members individually. (Pleasingly, groups of three always reach a majority decision!)This type of decision-making exercise draws on basic as well as advanced collaborative skills.

# Double-entry journals in action

| Key Stage: **KS3** | Subject / Topic: **Music** | Estimated duration: **30 mins** |
|---|---|---|

Miss Decibel's Year 8 Music class is studying samba music, as part of a cultural understanding project in their Music lesson. She splits the class into heterogeneous groups of three (one lower, one middle and one higher ability student). She then hands out a text which explains the origins of samba – how Brazil was colonised by the Portuguese and slaves were shipped from Africa, bringing with them their musical traditions.

After reading the text in silence, the students are asked to draw a vertical line in the middle of a page in their exercise book. Miss Decibel tells them to identify and list the 10 key events in the history of samba music (according to the text). On the right-hand side of the line, students write down their personal reaction to and interpretation of each event.

Finally, the groups study what each member wrote in response to the text. First of all, they look for common views (ideas about the source material that they all share). Next, the groups look for other ideas that they may not have individually thought of but that they unanimously agree with. They are now able to come up with a list which will form the basis of an analytical summary of the origins of samba music.

# What if...? and the PMI method

Higher-order questions that require learners to analyse, evaluate and design often make for successful group work stimuli. Questions starting with *'What if...?'* have the power to unlock the most sophisticated thinking processes. Think about the different cognitive levels required to answer these two questions:

1. *'Should we legalise performance enhancing drugs in sport?'*
2. *'What if we were to legalise performance enhancing drugs in sport?'*

The first question demands a 'yes / no' answer, whereas the second encourages students to weigh up the pros and cons and operate in hypothetical mode.

*'What if...?'* questions demand deep, divergent thinking and are a real treat for collaborative learners to feast on. Each group member can bring their individual perspective to bear.

When you plan a *'What if...?'* question as a stimulus for group work, a **PMI** grid is the perfect companion – a deep thinking tool that encourages collaboration and helps students to organise their ideas.

# What if…? and PMI in action

| Key Stage: **KS4** | Subject / Topic: **PSHE** | Estimated duration: **30+ mins** |
| --- | --- | --- |

PMI stands for *Plus*, *Minus* and *Interesting* (or *Implications*) and a PMI grid lists these in three columns. The *Plus* column refers to the positives or benefits; the *Minus* column to the negatives or downsides; and column three provides a space for the group to record anything they would be interested to know about the question posed (*Interesting*); or to list potential outcomes (*Implications*).

Taking the drugs in sport example, pupils could work in groups of four or five, with 15 minutes to listen to and note down each other's views, eg:

| PLUS | MINUS | INTERESTING |
| --- | --- | --- |
| Better performance of athletes | Dangerous for athletes' health | How far would athletes be prepared to go? |
| Cheaper because we would not need to test them | Performance depends on the effect of the drug taken and not athletes' effort | Would sport fans lose interest? |

Each group would then feed back to the class and compare findings. You could go on to compile a list of all *Interesting* questions to address in follow-up homework or classwork.

# Graphic organisers

Graphic organisers are visual templates which help students to arrange their ideas. They support the learning process and generally focus on specific thinking skills such as comparison, sequencing or problem-solving. When used in a collaborative context, graphic organisers offer a real chance to promote effective group interaction.

Although many students still plan with paper and pen, new technology tools can be very helpful because they allow easy editing. There is a multitude of teaching resources websites offering blank mind maps and graphic organisers for you to adapt to your teaching needs. Some are listed in the resources section at the end of this book.

Graphic organisers provide groups of pupils with a framework. They set well defined task boundaries and so encourage a task-centred approach to co-operative learning. Examples like the **fishbone map** allow pupils to explore the multiple causes of a problem.

# Graphic organisers

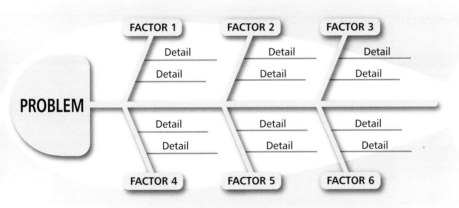

FACTOR 1

Detail

Detail

FACTOR 2

Detail

Detail

FACTOR 3

Detail

Detail

PROBLEM

Detail

Detail

Detail

Detail

Detail

Detail

FACTOR 4

FACTOR 5

FACTOR 6

# Graphic organisers in action

| Key Stage: | Subject / Topic: | Estimated duration: |
|---|---|---|
| **KS2** | **London 2012 Olympic Games** | **30 mins** |

Mr Wingold's Year 6 class is currently working on a cross-curricular project – *'2012: an Olympic Year for London'*. He wants his pupils to understand the factors that contributed to the success of the 2012 Games. He sets them a **group research task** based on Prime Minister David Cameron's words after the Games: *'You only need two words to sum up these Games: Britain delivered'*.

To provide a framework for the collaborative task, Mr Wingold designs an A3 **fishbone diagram** (see next page) on which he identifies four major success factors: the infrastructures, the athletes, the volunteers and the public.

He divides his pupils into four groups of six and hands out a template to each, along with an information pack containing information about the four success factors. Each member takes a turn to read out some facts. The group extracts key points about the success factors and adds them under the relevant headings on their template. Mr Wingold walks around the classroom, offers advice and assesses each group's performance.

# Mr Wingold's template

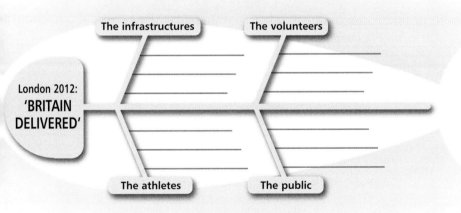

London 2012: 'BRITAIN DELIVERED'

The infrastructures

The volunteers

The athletes

The public

# Other useful graphic organisers

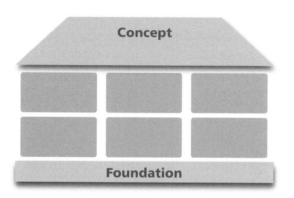

**Building blocks: a concept visualisation method**
The foundation rectangle represents the initial building stage without which the concept would not be able to stand. Resting firmly on the foundation block, the wall bricks constitute secondary construction elements. Finally the concept itself, visible and predominant, is represented as the roof of the building.

# Other useful graphic organisers

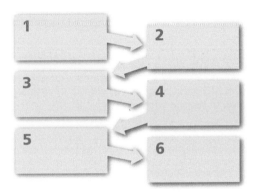

**Venn diagram**
This organiser is helpful when you want the group to quickly split information into areas of similarity and exclusivity. The two circles have a joint area to list commonalities while the rest is for differences or incompatibilities.

**The sequence chain**
This diagram allows students to organise information sequentially.

# Map it in groups!

**Mind mapping** or **concept mapping** is a powerful accelerated learning technique used to outline and classify information and ideas. Ideally suited to the visual learner, these graphical tools will help your students to make notes using single words, pictures or short phrases.

To make a mind map, start in the middle of a blank page with the title (main idea), and work outwards in all directions, producing a growing and organised structure made up of key words and concepts. Eventually, your diagram will show connections between elements of a topic and allow you to see the 'big picture'.

# Map it in groups!

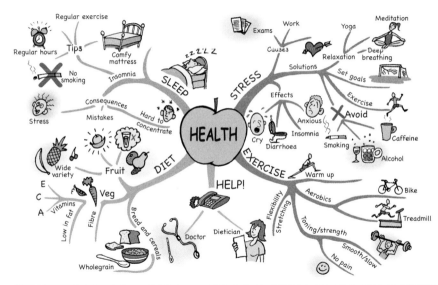

# Map it in groups!

Mind maps have numerous applications. In collaborative learning, they support groups in gathering, comparing and developing their thoughts.

| Group Application | Description |
|---|---|
| Task and Group Organisation | The task is written in the centre of the mind map. Responsibilities or sub-tasks are mapped and then allocated to group members. |
| Generating Ideas | Group members are given a topic. Together they brainstorm ideas and show connections between them. |
| Preparing a Presentation | The group has to deliver an unscripted presentation to the class. They 'map out' key points and use their diagram as a prompt. |
| Summarising / Group Plenary | Once a topic has been taught, group members work collaboratively to summarise key points on a mind map. |
| Organising Exam Revision | Group mind mapping can help with study skills. Students in groups identify priorities, key facts and useful revision tools. Those with poor study skills benefit most from the outcome – a clear revision agenda. |
| Tackling Controversial Issues | In Science, the class is divided into a pro-nuclear group and an anti-nuclear group. Each is given a study pack and time to read it. Group A mind-maps the positives and Group B the negatives. Both present their findings. Having heard both sides of the argument, students make an informed decision: are they for or against nuclear energy? |

# Limitations of group mind mapping

You may have noticed that most of the applications for mind mapping listed apply to more advanced learners, possibly at KS3, KS4 or KS5. Group conceptualisation demands a high degree of competency and solicits the use of **advanced collaborative skills** (pages 52–53) that younger learners are yet to acquire.

Mind mapping mimics the thought process of an individual (or group of individuals). Less structured and more anarchic than other strategies described in this chapter, it requires a real focus on the task and its outcome.

Despite the limitations of this strategy, students can become totally engrossed in group mind mapping. I recently observed a Year 9 class so absorbed in their mind mapping task that they 'forgot' to take their morning break at the end of the lesson. A rare and priceless occurrence.

# Conclusion

The *quick and easy* group activities described in this section can be easily incorporated within a wider lesson structure. These 'free-standing' strategies are meant to support your teaching objectives without taking over the whole lesson. They constitute a brick in your teaching edifice.

The kind of group work we've looked at benefits your students on many different levels. Firmly rooted in your learners' ZPD – where individual members bring their own talents and knowledge to the group – these strategies permit the development of basic (and some more advanced) collaborative skills. When carefully run and regularly practised, they discourage free-riding behaviour and encourage an inclusive classroom ethos.

Effective collaborative strategies will eventually push most reluctant learners out of their 'comfort' zone, an area usually located at the back of the classroom, near the radiator with great views over the basketball court.

# High Impact
# Strategies

# Introduction

So far this book has made the case for collaborative learning and provided you with the knowledge and tools to have a go. Before moving on to look at full collaborative models, you are encouraged to press pause and reflect.

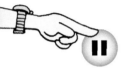

- How important is collaborative learning to the **development** of my learners?
- What are the **benefits** of classroom co-operation?
- What **outcomes** can I expect?
- What **skills** do I need / want my learners to develop to be successful in a collaborative context?
- How can I **plan** effectively for collaborative learning? (group size and composition, resources, etc)

The following pages present and illustrate five high impact collaborative strategies. When carefully planned and implemented, they deliver outstanding results in terms of knowledge acquisition and skills development.

# 1. Carousel

Carousels are a fun way for your students to experience a wide range of activities based around an area of study. Divide the class into mixed ability groups of no more than five.

Groups rotate around the classroom, stopping at various 'stations' for a designated period of time (typically 5 -10 minutes). Each 'station' carries a separate activity and each activity focuses on different skills. Carousel activities could include:

- A **reading comprehension** with a printed text as a stimulus. This could be a true or false exercise, a questionnaire on the text, a summary to produce, etc
- A **listening comprehension** with an audio recording as a stimulus
- A **speaking exercise** where, for example, students take it in turn to present their thoughts on a picture or a quotation. They can then synthesise their group thoughts into a first person plural paragraph ('*we believe that...*')
- A **creative writing** activity based on the topical knowledge that they have acquired so far
- A **learning game** (match up activity, crossword, board game with a dice, guess who, etc...)
- An **interactive activity** on the IWB
- A **mind map** or a **graphic organiser** to fill in

# 1. Carousel

## Skills & learning objectives

Carousel lessons are useful for:
- Developing group autonomy and shared ownership
- Encouraging peer support and minimising the degree of direct teacher intervention
- Revising a unit of work through a wide range of table activities

## Resources

- Your students need pen and paper (or their exercise books) to take notes. Alternatively, you can place worksheets at each 'station'
- You need a whistle or other loud instrument to signal rotation of activities and a timer to ensure the exact amount of time is spent at each 'station'. If your classroom is equipped with an interactive whiteboard, use a free online stopwatch or countdown timer. Failing that, a kitchen timer with a loud ring does the trick

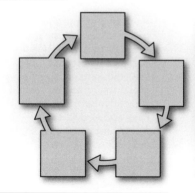

# 1. Carousel

**Benefits and pitfalls**

The success of this type of lesson lies in strictly adhering to timing. A steady pace and a healthy sense of competition will help maintain student interest.

Select straightforward activities which demand minimal instructions. This will ensure groups do not waste time trying to work out what to do. If instructions are needed, print them out on a card placed in the centre of the table. If your lesson is supported by another adult (or older students working as helpers), post them strategically at a station where assistance is likely to be needed.

Carousels are pacey, competitive and fun, but they require a lot of preparation. Share the workload by getting together with colleagues in your subject area or teaching phase and planning the lesson together.

If you have concerns about behaviour, you can minimise the potential for disruption between activities by going for **static carousels**, where the tasks rather than the students rotate.

# Carousel lesson step-by-step

1. Rearrange the tables in your classroom so that your pupils can sit in groups of four. Ask the pupils to line up outside the classroom and call them in in alphabetical order. Allocate a table number to each name ('*Sonia is on table 4, Kiran goes to table 5...*'). This is also the number of the group that they belong to for the duration of the carousel lesson. Ensure that students are in the right place before giving whole class instructions.

2. State your learning objectives. Explain the carousel procedure and tell your students how long they have at each station. Add an optional competitive element (eg a prize to win, gold/ silver/ bronze medal or a no-homework pass). Inform pupils that all tasks should be completed in their exercise books, unless otherwise stated in the table instructions, and labelled according to their station number.

3. The lesson is 60 minutes long and there are six different stations. Each group will spend seven minutes on each activity. The first minute of each seven-minute slot is devoted to reading the printed instructions in silence. All team members should be clear about what they are expected to do and that responsibility lies within the group.

# Carousel lesson step-by-step

4.  After one minute silent reading, students start the activity and should complete it within the allocated time. Blow the whistle every 7 minutes. Each group moves to the next table for their next task. The process continues until everyone has worked on all the tasks.

5.  In the last 10 -15 minutes of the lesson, bring your class together for feedback and review of the learning objectives. Encourage pupils to reflect on individual areas of strength (when they helped their group the most, for instance) and areas for improvement (when they relied on other members to help them). If you have used the carousel strategy to revise and practise before an end-of-topic test, ask them to rate their knowledge of the topic and to set themselves home revision targets.

    You can also focus your lesson review on the process of co-operative learning: how well did they get on with the task as a group? Which group work skills did they use? How can they work even better together next time? Alternatively, ask them to fill in a self-evaluation sheet or a group evaluation questionnaire for plenary or homework (see pages 123 and 125 for examples).

# 2. Speed talking

Speed talking is the educational answer to speed dating… if only in terms of room layout. The purpose is to reinforce learning via simple peer interaction. Speed talking is effectively pair work with multiple partners.

The process is straightforward. Arrange the tables in a horseshoe, with facing chairs on either side. Split your class into two groups of equal size. Group A sits on the outer rim of the horseshoe opposite group B on the inner. All students in group A get to 'chat' with everyone in group B, and vice versa. Before modelling the task, ensure that each student has a partner opposite him or her.

Students talk to each other in pairs, swapping partners at regular time intervals. When their time is up, students in group B move up to the next seat and start a new conversation with a 'static' student from group A. Pace is important. 'Speed talkers' get a set amount of time to practise a skill or find out the required information from each other.

Some students may feel uncomfortable about the whole 'dating' aspect, so it may be best to play down the speed dating parallel.

# 2. Speed talking

## Skills & learning objectives

Speed talking is useful for:
- Understanding multiple perspectives on an issue
- Gathering information about a specific topic (in conjunction with a mind map or graphic organiser to take notes)
- Practising speaking and interview skills
- Encouraging peer support and minimising direct teacher intervention

## Resources

- A timer to measure intervals
- A whistle or a loud instrument to signal rotation
- Students may need pen and paper to take notes
- A **prompt card** containing questions or headings to use during the speed talk can help reduce the risk of digression and ensure that the conversation remains on track

# 2. Speed talking

## Benefits and pitfalls

Speed talking is an engaging group activity that promotes independent learning. It has applications in a wide range of subjects, eg:

- In Modern Foreign Languages, it gives pupils a great opportunity to practise pronunciation, vocabulary and fluency
- In Maths, learners can use speed talking to quiz each other on key mathematical vocabulary
- Across the range of subjects it can be used as a peer assessment tool or revision technique

Teacher modelling is an important preparatory phase with this technique. Students shouldn't just *hear* about how speed talking works, they should *see* it in action! Show them how to do it.

Once underway, the speed talking lesson has to flow without teacher intervention. The pace has to be rhythmic and sustained (change partners every three to five minutes). All you need to do is facilitate and supervise the process, assessing its impact on individuals as well as the whole class. Allow time at the end for that all-important debrief.

# Speed talking – a sample lesson

A secondary school in north-east England uses speed talking in its Citizenship programme to raise questions about individual responsibilities towards homelessness and poverty.

Before the lesson starts the teacher rearranges his classroom for a speed talking lesson with 30 students. He organises the tables in an 'S'-shape.

**First 15 minutes**
Students are divided into A's and B's. They sit opposite a partner at a table – A's on the outside of the 'S' and the B's on the inside. As an initial stimulus for discussion, the teacher tells the class, they will be listening to the song *Another Day in Paradise*, (Phil Collins, 1989). They are given the lyrics on an A4 sheet but the teacher makes a point of not telling them anything about the meaning of the song. He explains the learning objectives:

- To understand the issue raised by the song
- To discuss the notion of individual responsibility
- To suggest solutions to the problem

He then plays the song and students are encouraged to annotate the sheet with initial ideas.

# Speed talking – a sample lesson

**15 – 30 minutes**
Group A students are given a list of around 20 **open questions** (*eg What is this song about? How do you know? Do you agree with the line…? Why the title?*) The teacher demonstrates how group A should conduct the interview and encourages them to take notes and not to ask the same questions every time. The interviews begin. Every three minutes, the teacher blows the whistle and all interviewees (B's) move seats to be quizzed by the next interviewer.

**30 – 45 minutes**
The process is repeated but this time A's and B's swap roles.

**45 – 60 minutes**
The teacher blows the whistle three times to signals the end of the activity. He now orchestrates a whole-class feedback session where views and ideas are shared. The teacher enquires about differing personal interpretations of the song. On a *PowerPoint* slide, he then reveals factual information about homelessness in the UK. For homework, students are asked to research the issue further in preparation for a piece of writing discussing the notion of individual responsibility and suggesting solutions to the problem of homelessness.

# 3. Reversed objective

The reversed objective lesson focuses on analysing the process of creating a product. The lesson is designed and conducted 'backwards', from the finished product to the initial design stage. Learners in groups 'travel back' to the source, analyse the materials and tools used, discuss success criteria, time constraints, etc. Once the **finished product** has been 'scrutinised' and 'dismantled', students are able to create their own version of it.

The finished product can be concrete or abstract and can be presented orally or in writing. Fundamentally, it acts as a **model** for your pupils to recreate:

A cushion in Textiles     An item of packaging in Business Studies     Software in IT

A newspaper article in History     A model essay in English     A painting in Art

A weather report in Geography     An experiment in Science

Reversed objective lessons are conducted in groups of three to six students. Tables are arranged with enough desk space to create a comfortable work station for each group. For more complex tasks, you may decide on competency grouping rather than heterogeneous. While all four basic collaborative skills are at work in a reversed objective lesson, it is the use of more advanced skills like negotiation, persuasion, evaluation and synthesis that contributes to the success of the task.

# 3. Reversed objective

**Skills & learning objectives**

The reversed objective lesson is useful for:
* Developing decision-making and problem-solving skills in a collaborative context
* Activating prior knowledge and gathering relevant information in order to analyse, evaluate and create
* Focusing on the various stages of the creative process

**Resources**

* A **finished product** to study
* An accompanying worksheet and/or set of printed instructions
* Your students need pen, paper, a long ruler (for plans and drawings), their class notes and textbooks

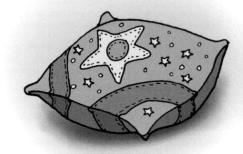

# 3. Reversed objective

## Benefits and pitfalls

Due to their problem solving nature, reversed objective lessons are highly engaging for learners who enjoy a challenge. The key is to persuade your students that the deconstruction of a quality product is a useful step towards creating their own version of it. Encourage your students to identify themselves with detectives or spies. Use the language of a private investigator when explaining the task, *'Look how we can pull this apart, uncover its secrets and use them to our advantage!'* Build a sense of expectation and let your students take the credit for solving the task!

 The higher the number of students in the group, the more difficult it is to ensure everyone's full involvement in the task so try to limit groups to no more than four. With groups of five or six, there is a greater risk of friction, and *free-riders* can get away with it more easily!

# Reversed objective lesson – step-by-step

1. Prior to the lesson, split your class into mixed ability groups of three to six. Students sit in their allocated groups at tables with plenty of work space. They begin with a short quiz (or other knowledge review starter) to recap on the previous week's lesson. This helps the group to bond and encourages them to 'think together' from the outset.

2. After whole-class marking of the starter activity, introduce the **finished product** that will be the focus for your reversed objective lesson (examples on page 93). Give your students a few minutes to familiarise themselves with the product, examine it, discuss its use and, most importantly, assess its **quality**! What makes it a *good* product? Encourage them to share their initial thoughts about it in their groups. Then, get your students to brainstorm subject-specific success criteria. Discuss them openly with the class. At this stage, share the objectives of your reversed lesson with the class:

   *'Today we will be looking at what makes a great essay / musical composition / advertising campaign / food recipe / design, etc.'*

   Explain that you intend to use a **deconstruction** method to find out how to create a product of similar quality.

# Reversed objective – step-by-step

3.  One English department in a large secondary school uses the reversed objective method to study effective essay writing at GCSE. Students work in groups of six to deconstruct an A⁺ essay. One pair within the group analyses the language (style, register, vocabulary). Another pair looks at the content (examples/ evidence, development of ideas, personal views). The third pair examines the essay's structure (paragraph construction and sequence, introduction, main body, conclusion). Each pair in turn feeds back to the team. Finally, the group works together to draw up a list of the skills and knowledge required to produce an equally good piece of writing.

4.  Spend some time with each group to check that they have come to the 'right' conclusions. Once satisfied with the outcome of the deconstruction phase, introduce and explain the final stage of the reversed objective lesson, the **creation** phase. Students now understand the process involved in constructing a quality product and should be able to create one themselves (either independently for homework, or collaboratively in class). They will have a mental (and hopefully written) checklist of 'quality criteria' to refer to as they design their own product.

# 4. Jigsaw learning

The jigsaw learning technique created by Elliot Aronson in 1971 works in three steps:

1. Students are placed into heterogeneous 'home' groups.
2. They are divided into new groups to become experts on a topic.
3. The experts return to their home group to share their findings with the other members.

Take the example of a chemistry assignment where 25 students have to research five different forms of power generation (nuclear, solar, hydroelectric, fossil fuel, wind). Students begin in home groups of five. Each group member draws, or is given, one of the five topics to be studied. New groups are then formed – all those who drew nuclear make up a new group of five; all those who drew solar form a group, and so on.

There are now five 'expert' groups. Each group is given a task or range of tasks to complete within a given time. They work together to develop expertise in the topic. Experts then return to their home groups, pooling their knowledge to tackle the difficult question of how much importance should be given to each method of power generation.

Utilise all the space available in your classroom. Spread groups out around clusters of tables with room to spread out individual notes and resources.

# 4. Jigsaw learning

**Skills & learning objectives**

The jigsaw technique is useful for:
* Promoting positive student interdependence and minimising the degree of direct teacher intervention
* Developing active listening and speaking skills with a view to facilitating the transfer of knowledge from learner to learner

**Resources**

* Students need pen and paper (or their exercise book) to take notes
* If necessary, a help sheet / set of instructions

Source material (websites, articles, graphs, charts, textbooks, brochures, etc) subdivided in study sections according to the number and nature of your expert groups.

# 4. Jigsaw learning

**Benefits and pitfalls**

Jigsaw learning is the perfect marriage between independent enquiry and peer development. Learners who become experts have a dual responsibility. Their first duty is to increase their level of competence in a particular field. To gain the expertise required, they mainly use intrapersonal and active listening skills (reading and listening around the topic, working out sequences, taking notes and summarising, etc). Their second responsibility is to *tell* others in their home group about their findings. Here they employ interpersonal and speaking skills to ensure the information is appropriately passed on.

Some students may feel anxious about taking on what they perceive to be an intimidating level of responsibility. Worried they might not understand it themselves, they dread the prospect of instructing others about their allocated field of expertise.

To avoid a meltdown, provide pupils with a bank of written statements to help them talk to their home group with more clarity (*'Initially, I thought that…'; 'I have now found out that…'; 'I realised that…'; ' the pros and the cons are…'; 'my conclusions are…'*). You can also show them how to organise the information in sections so that they can process it more easily.

# Jigsaw learning – a sample lesson *

- A Year 6 teacher wants her pupils to be able to define the fairy tale genre. She divides them into five 'home' groups with five pupils in each group

- Each group is presented with five classic fairy tales: *The Little Mermaid, Jack and the Beanstalk, Pinocchio, Hansel and Gretel, Aladdin and the Magic Lamp*

- Individual pupils in each group are given one of the fairy tales to read in silence. Once they have read it, they are split into expert groups: one person from each home group joins a new group comprising all those allocated the same fairy tale

- Each expert group is given a questionnaire on their allocated fairy tale

1. *Who are the characters? Who is the hero? Who is the villain?*
2. *Where does the story take place?*
3. *What are the main events of the story?*
4. *Are there any magical or supernatural events? If so, what are they?*
5. *What happens in the end?*
6. *How does the story make you feel?*

*Inspired by Ellen Berg's account of her jigsaw lesson (http://www.educationworld.com/a_curr/curr324.shtml)

# Jigsaw learning – a sample lesson *

- Once the questions have been discussed and answered, the home groups are reconvened. Members share their findings

- Each home group has to produce an A3 poster to explain what all five fairy tales have in common. They also have to write their own definition of the genre based on the outcomes of their comparative research

- Posters are displayed at the front of the class. The teacher reads out the textbook definition of a fairy tale. She points out to her students how similar the definition is to their own conclusions

- During the whole-class plenary discussion, the teacher draws up a list of conventions attached to the genre. Finally, she sets her pupils a creative writing task to create their own original fairy tale

*Inspired by Ellen Berg's account of her jigsaw lesson
(http://www.educationworld.com/a_curr/curr324.shtml)

# 5. Dragons' Den – pitch your ideas

***Dragons' Den*** follows the pattern of the popular TV show of the same name, where entrepreneurs pitch their business concepts to millionaires willing to invest their own cash. It is a high-powered collaborative strategy with well-defined roles, differentiated outcomes and a competitive dimension. Students learn how to 'pitch' ideas and persuade an audience.

*   The **entrepreneurs** present their idea, product or concept to the *Dragons*. They have to use a wide range of skills and factual information to convince the panel to invest in them
*   The **investors** (or *Dragons*) have to challenge the entrepreneurs. They ask questions, draw conclusions and assess the viability of the concept presented to them. They will only invest in one team, so their assessment has to be rigorous

Divide your students into two distinct categories: entrepreneurs and investors. The ideal group size is four to five. Entrepreneurs will compete against each other for the investors' prize. Consider placing more able pupils in the investors' group: their role tends to be more challenging – less structured and more responsive. At the front of the classroom place a row of chairs behind a couple of large tables for the *Dragons* to watch and listen to the auditions. Groups of tables are scattered around the room for each team to prepare their pitch.

# 5. Dragons' Den – pitch your ideas

## Skills & learning objectives

The *Dragons' Den* technique is useful for:
- Learning how to put a strong argument forward (entrepreneurs)
- Setting and applying rigorous assessment criteria (investors)
- Employing and deploying the full range of collaborative skills

ACHOO!

## Resources

- Access to a selected range of information, eg textbooks, notes, internet, etc. Entrepreneurs will need to convince with facts not just wit
- Teams of entrepreneurs will also need to think of creative and visual ways to 'pitch' (PowerPoint, mind map on a flip chart, photos, poster, a role play, a musical performance, etc)
- Time – allow ample preparation and rehearsal time for both entrepreneurs and investors. The success of the task depends primarily on the quality of the students' groundwork before the pitch

# 5. Dragons' Den – pitch your ideas

## Benefits and pitfalls

In the business sense of the word, 'to pitch' means to promote a product in front of a panel. Therefore the main advantage of this concept is its adaptability to a range of topics and applications in all aspects of the curriculum. In Geography, for instance, you might want to use *Dragons' Den* as a revision method for the latest unit of work on earthquakes. You could ask your entrepreneurs to pitch a new plan for a region affected by regular seismic activity. In a Dance lesson, students in groups could pitch an original composition in front of a team of judges who will use set criteria to assess their performance, etc.

However, *Dragons' Den* demands a fair amount of preparation and planning, both on your behalf and your students'. Entrepreneurs must take a lot into consideration before putting together their pitch. They need to identify roles within the team and think of a strong structure for their pitch (eg a three-part introduction / development / conclusion set-up). Investors have an even more complex task on their hands. Prior to the pitch they need to decide on possible lines of enquiry. They also need to familiarise themselves in advance with the success criteria they have designed together, or that you have provided for them.

# Dragons' Den – a sample lesson

Year 5 have been learning about the moon in their Science lessons. The teacher splits the class into teams for their collaborative task: planning a trip to the moon. The winning team will be the one who designs the best spacecraft, packs the most useful items and, most importantly, convinces the panel of the importance of their unique scientific mission!

Four teams of 5 entrepreneurs will be competing. All members have to speak during each team's five minutes pitch. The panel of investors is made up of pupils who are keen scientists and/or high achievers.

The teacher gives the class 40 minutes to prepare. The investors sit together and work out a list of questions to ask (*'What will your mission be? Why is it so important? What will the spacecraft be made of?'* etc). They also discuss success criteria. The teacher assists them in creating an evaluation sheet which will allow them to choose the winning project.

# Dragons' Den – a sample lesson

The four teams of entrepreneurs use their preparation time to plan their unique mission to the moon. They are allowed to look up information in their science textbook but they cannot discuss their project outside their team. In addition, they have to come up with a diagram to illustrate their mission. In the last ten minutes before the pitch, they plan their intervention together: who says what, at what point, etc.

All four teams present their project and are thoroughly quizzed by the investors. After each pitch, the investors fill in their evaluation sheet together. The panel retires to deliberate. The winning mission is finally chosen and the reward is a well-deserved multi-million pound virtual investment!

*Dragons' Den* lessons are popular with pupils. Try thinking of other TV or radio panel / game shows that could provide a framework for collaborative learning. There are endless possibilities!

# Range of applications

The high impact strategies outlined in this section have shown the value of approaches to learning that promote talk and interaction.

However, the list provided is far from exhaustive, and knowing when to use which strategy depends on the aims and desired outcomes of your lesson. Below and on the following pages are five possible **applications** for collaborative learning:

Ordering and sequencing

Revision

Problem-solving

Collaborative creation

Debating

# Ordering and sequencing

Group activities for ordering and sequencing include the card game *'Higher or Lower?'* Create your own set of cards with pieces of information (one on each card) for pupils to rank in order of importance, chronology, value, etc. Place them face down in a pile at the centre of your pupils' table. Pupils in their group turn each card over, one at a time, and place them in the right sequence; from the least to the most, the lowest to the highest, etc. A History teacher might, for example, prepare 10 cards on events that led to the American Civil War and ask students to classify them in chronological order.

**Diamond ranking activities** also involve pupils sorting ideas in order of importance. Place key words, statements or pictures on nine cards. Learners then place them in order of importance: what they feel is most important goes on the top, followed by a row of two not quite as important below, then three, and another two that are less important and finally the least important is placed at the bottom, creating a diamond shape.

Ordering and sequencing activities make use of basic collaborative skills and don't need much input from you. They can, however, lead to disagreements and, unless supplemented with an analytical task, may only provide superficial understanding of a concept.

# Revision

Collaborative learning can support effective study skills. The **conveyer belt technique**, for example, is an information-handling strategy which focuses on breadth of knowledge. It requires learners in an assembly line to take it in turn to work on a group assignment. Students in pairs sit opposite each other somewhere along the 'conveyer belt' (a line of tables in the classroom). Each pair is given a piece of information to study. The information is discussed, processed and placed back onto the 'conveyer belt' for the next pair to add to it.

In literary subjects, GCSE teachers use it to revise essay writing skills. A selection of essay titles travels down the line at regular intervals in the lesson. Each pair contributes information to a blank essay plan, which is then passed on to the next pair who has to add more detail.

By the end of the lesson, students have tackled a wide range of essay titles. They benefit from reading the input of others in the class, which they get to discuss, assess, criticise and improve in pairs.

# Problem-solving

Problem-solving tasks call for higher-level reasoning and a good set of collaborative skills. They tend to work better with experienced group learners. They can be highly engaging but can also consume a lot of lesson time. The more engaged your pupils are, the more heated the discussion can be. If consensus is difficult to achieve, facilitate the process by modelling critical evaluation skills.

A good activity to practise problem-solving skills is the **mystery lesson**. Pupils are expected to investigate a central question that has more than one reasonable answer ('*Why did Alice follow the rabbit down the hole?*' would make a good mystery question).

The 'clues' needed to answer the question are presented on separate slips of paper that your pupils need to analyse, sort, link, evaluate, synthesise, etc.

# Collaborative creation

Group interaction can help get the creative juices flowing. Bring your pupils together and ask them to come up with something new, eg:

- A piece of artwork
- An article for the school magazine
- A costume for a drama production
- A PE fitness programme
- The ending of a short story
- A new design for the teachers' staffroom

Collaborative creation develops your pupils' spirit of enterprise and gives them a great sense of autonomy. Because of its open-ended and time-consuming nature, collaborative creation requires careful planning. Bear in mind, too, that some children can be over-ambitious and overlook obstacles.

# Debating

Debating, which helps improve argument and persuasive skills, is most effective in groups of four or six. Split the group in two equal teams: those in favour of a view and those against it. The question to debate has to be broad enough for a range of opinions to be expressed. Students may be asked to adopt a point of view which is not their own; therefore they need to be able to distance themselves from the key question to debate.

Stay away from sensitive issues that may affect children personally. Good preliminary research and open-mindedness form the basis of a meaningful debate. Your students need to be prepared to assess the process on its own merits rather than on their agreement or disagreement with the views expressed.

# Conclusion

> 'Tell me
> and I'll forget;
> Show me
> and I'll remember;
> Involve me
> and I'll understand.'

This Chinese proverb says more about teaching than many academic publications on the subject. Most learners would agree with it. In class, they want to be *involved* in the learning process, not just *told* something. Why would anyone want to be at the receiving end of a process they have no control over, like some sort of battery farmed hen?

This proverb also builds a strong case for collaborative learning. **Collective involvement** (through shared ownership of the learning process) is the powerful common denominator in all the ideas presented in this Pocketbook. None of these strategies can work without participation from each and every learner in the group. The formula for collaborative success is in fact a simple one: the higher the degree of personal participation, the more likely it is that the strategy will produce positive results.

So let's close down the battery farm and get those hens roaming around instead!

The Power of
More Than
One

Planning for
Collaborative
Learning

Collaborative
Learning
Starter Pack

High Impact
Strategies

**Assessing and
Evaluating**

# Assessing
# and Evaluating

# An impossible task?

We've looked at the benefits and practicalities of group work, but what about assessing it? When asked about issues that they associate with group work, teachers often comment:

*'How can I tell who accounts for how much of the success of the task?'*

Measuring individual accountability is perceived as problematic. Problematic, maybe, but not impossible.

# Piña collaborada

Imagine this: on a Saturday night out with friends, you treat yourself to a delicious cocktail. It looks great and tastes amazing, but you struggle to pinpoint the exact ingredients, their proportion, provenance, flavour-enhancing properties, etc. The cocktail tastes far better than any of its components would if they were taken separately.

This also applies to the success of a collaborative task. Even though individual contributions can be hard to quantify, this doesn't necessarily have an adverse effect on the quality of outcome. In the first place, the impact of a collaborative task should be measured **at a group level**.

**The group is accountable for the success of the task and each member is accountable for the success of the group.**

This is an important message that you should constantly reiterate to your collaborative class (particularly when your students are not yet experienced in this method of learning, as you want to encourage co-operation rather than competition). Once co-operation is established, it is much easier to look at progress, commitment and attainment of individual students within the group.

# Assessing process and product

When assessing groups there's a distinction to make between **process** assessment and **product** assessment.

Process assessment focuses on evaluating collaborative skills; product assessment evaluates the outcome

To produce the most accurate picture, both types of assessment are needed but they don't have to take place at the same time. Although product assessment, by definition, has to be carried out once the task is completed, process assessment can be used part-way through the task in order to inform the team's progress.

Product assessment is summative; process assessment can be formative and summative

# Product assessment

Assessing the product involves using a clear set of criteria shared with the class from the outset. While your pupils are on task, regularly remind them of the **success criteria** (as explained on page 29). This will help ensure that they stay on course throughout the activity.

In less structured and more open-ended group tasks, nominate a *'monitor'* within each group to conduct a regular review of the learning objectives and to keep the group on track. Involving students in deciding what the success criteria are provides a clearer focus and direction. Display the criteria during the activity, either on the board or on a printed sheet handed out to each group.

Product assessment generally applies to the group's work rather than individual contributions. You can however ask individuals to write a **review** of their product (or another group's product) for homework. This should provide valuable information about their understanding of and contribution to the final outcome.

# Process assessment

Gaining a clear insight into the dynamics of a group can be a difficult task for the teacher-observer. When examining how a group interacts, make notes on key aspects such as engagement, leadership, ability to compromise, subdivision of tasks, perseverance, etc (see page 29 for success criteria). Devise your own grading system in your mark book. Award a score to each individual on specific collaborative learning skills and attitudes. Compare the results from one collaborative session to the next in order to assess the process both individually and at a group level.

Another way to evaluate the collaborative process is to ask teams and individuals to self- or peer-assess. In the plenary phase of your lesson, hand out an evaluation sheet or a questionnaire to complete. As far as skills assessment is concerned, this is the best way to gather evidence of progress. Examples are provided with guidance in the next few pages.

# Process assessment using group scores

Group scores can be awarded for effective collaboration. They allow you to evaluate team work without having to assess each member's contribution individually. Group scoring can bring teams together, although, like all competitive strategies, there is a risk of creating discouragement and friction. Consider how your groups are likely to react before pinning up your group scoreboard at the front of your classroom! If you use group scoring:

- Make it **transparent**. Discuss the scoring criteria with the class in advance
- Make it a **joint decision**. Involve your students in the planning process by asking them to draw up a list of which skills they think they should be scored on
- Make it **relevant**. Focus on a collaborative skill – basic or advanced – which they need to improve on as a group, or implement as the next step in their group development
- Make it **visible**. Display a group scoreboard in the classroom, so that all teams get to see their progress as well as the progress of others. Ranking highly on the group scoreboard can act as a strong motivator, particularly with younger learners

# Pupil self-evaluation

Self-evaluation takes on an extra dimension in collaborative work. Students who self-evaluate gauge their understanding and progress against a set of standards, but also against the others in their group. Therefore, effective self-evaluation is at the core of all group learning activities.

Self-evaluation sheets like the one on page 123 allow your students to reflect on their contribution as well as that of others in the group. Before asking your students to complete a self-evaluation, teach them about the four basic collaborative skills (intrapersonal, interpersonal, active listening and speaking). Demonstrate how much of an impact they have on the outcome of a group task. You could even film your groups at work and use the footage to highlight skills deficiency and identify positive contributions. Students will get to see what *'helping the group'* looks like in practice.

Once your class is familiar with the set of standards (the four basic collaborative skills), self-evaluation becomes a much more purposeful exercise and starts to prompt self-improvement.

# Example of pupil self-evaluation sheet

Name ................................................... Date ....... / ....... / ...........

## Title of the task

What did you do to help the group?

What did other people do to help the group?

What else could you do to improve your contribution?

What else could the group do to improve?

How much did you enjoy the task? (circle the right one) 😊 😐 ☹

# Group evaluation

To hone their collaborative skills, learners need opportunities to **practise** as well as to **reflect**.

Group review (or group evaluation) plays an important part in ensuring the development and consolidation of work teams, particularly when it comes to long-established ones. Students who have been working together for a length of time will benefit most from an end-of-lesson group evaluation task like the questionnaire on the next page. Their familiarity with each other increases their confidence to discuss openly issues such as participation, perseverance, fairness and responsibility.

With group evaluation, beware the dominance of members who – wittingly or unwittingly – impose their views on the group. *'I'd say that everyone was treated the same in the group. Is everyone ok with that?'* If you anticipate problems such as this, lead and manage the discussion yourself to facilitate group reflection. Group evaluation gives you insight into the effectiveness of your collaborative learners' relationships. It reveals the strength of the glue holding the components of the group together.

# Example of group evaluation questionnaire

Team Name: ........................ Title of group activity: ......................................................

Read the 10 statements below and tick true or false. You must **all agree** within your team If you cannot agree unanimously, simply tick the last column (no consensus).

Please bear in mind that there is no right or wrong answer; you just need to discuss each statement as a group and come to a decision on what to tick. There is a question at the end which will help you reflect on how to get even better as a group. Thank you in advance for your honesty.

**Statement**

|  | true | false | no consensus |
|---|---|---|---|
| 1. We all took part in the activity | ☐ | ☐ | ☐ |
| 2. We knew what to do | ☐ | ☐ | ☐ |
| 3. We knew how to do it | ☐ | ☐ | ☐ |
| 4. We are happy with the final decision / outcome | ☐ | ☐ | ☐ |
| 5. We all tried hard | ☐ | ☐ | ☐ |
| 6. Some tried harder than others | ☐ | ☐ | ☐ |
| 7. We listened to each other's opinions | ☐ | ☐ | ☐ |
| 8. We asked the teacher for help when we needed it | ☐ | ☐ | ☐ |
| 9. We treated everyone in the group fairly and equally | ☐ | ☐ | ☐ |
| 10. We enjoyed working as a group | ☐ | ☐ | ☐ |

*What do we need to do differently next time?*

Date:...............

# Conclusion

The positive impact of collaborative learning on student achievement is tied to the way you establish engaging group goals whilst requiring individual accountability. Thus, group members are given incentive and motivation to help one another through the task at hand. Research studies also point to other important benefits, such as inclusion and mutual respect. Relations between different ethnic groups are improved when individuals from diverse backgrounds are brought together to work in a respectful co-operative manner.

Rome was not built in a day, though. And it wasn't built by one person either. Collaborative learning takes a bit of time and practice. It is a brick-by-brick process which demands careful management, but what you gain in return far outweighs the initial investment.

As you close the door at the end of an invigorating day filled with classroom interaction and collaborative discussions, take a seat at your desk and reflect for a minute on the young people you have just taught. Independent learners with the ability to listen and be listened to, they are equipped with essential life skills that can be passed onto the next generation. Legacy is what teaching is all about; we teach to build the next Rome.

# Resources – books and websites

**Cooperative Learning in the Classroom: Putting it into Practice** by Wendy Jolliffe. Sage Publications Ltd, 2007

**Learning to Collaborate, Collaborating to Learn: Understanding and Promoting Educationally Productive Collaborative Work** by Littleton et al. Nova Biomedical, 2004

**Mind in Society: The Development of Higher Psychological Processes** by Lev Vygotsky. Harvard University Press, 1978

**Promoting Effective Group Work in the Primary Classroom** by Baines, Blatchford and Kutnick. Routledge, 2009

**Thought and Language** by Lev Vygotsky. MIT Press, 1986

**Vygotsky's Educational Theory in Cultural Context** (ed) Kozulin, et al. CUP, 2003

**www.edutopia.org/common-ground** (teaching pupils benefits of working together)

**www.teachingexpertise.com** (useful articles on group work)

**www.dailyteachingtools.com/cooperative-learning-grouping.html** (practical tips)

**www.thirteen.org/edonline/concept2class/coopcollab** (how using small, co-operative groups can help improve learning in class)

**www.jigsaw.org** (focuses on the implementation of jigsaw learning)

**www.educationscotland.gov.uk/learningteachingandassessment/approaches** (interesting section on classroom collaboration)

The following three sites offer free templates for mind-maps and graphic organisers:
**www.exploratree.org.uk     www.classtools.net     www.myt4l.com**

# About the author

**Gael Luzet**

Originally from France, Gael has been teaching in UK secondary schools since the late 1990's. He became an Advanced Skills Teacher in January 2006, is a mentor for newly qualified and trainee teachers and has worked as an external examiner for an ITT provider. He has led several professional networks on effective language teaching skills and Gifted & Talented education.

Since 2008 Gael has helped colleagues develop pupil participation and collaborative learning strategies in a wide range of primary and secondary schools. Now in charge of Teaching and Learning in a successful secondary school, he runs a CPD programme where he encourages teachers to implement practical and innovative ideas.

Recently, Gael was awarded Specialist Leader in Education status and now advises secondary school leaders on good practice in Teaching and Learning and MFL.

His own collaborative team includes his wife Cheryl, a great source of encouragement; his friend and ex-colleague Sarah, a trusted source of advice; and his two children Max and Mathilde who continue to be a fabulous source of distraction.